THE LORD GAVE THE WORD

A Study in the History of the Biblical Text

Malcolm H. Watts

Tyndale House, Dorset Road, London, SW19 3NN, England

20M/01/03
© Trinitarian Bible Society 1998

Contents

The Old Testament   1
The first language   1
Writing materials   2
Revelation   2
Twin doctrine   3
Written   4
The Originals   4
The Temple   4
Significance of the Ark   5
One Book   6
Copies   6
The work of scribes   7
Loss of the originals   7
The Great Synagogue   8
The Famous Massoretes   9
The Massoretic Text   10
Old Testament Summary   11

The New Testament   12
Christian truth written down   13
The Divine Originals   13
Accurate Copying   14
Textual Variants   15
Reproducing the authentic
    New Testament Text   16
The Surviving Greek manuscripts   17
    1. *Papyri*   17
    2. *Uncials*   18
    3. *Minuscules*   19
    4. *Lectionaries*   19
Classification   20
    A. *Byzantine Text-type*   21
    B. *The Alexandrian Text-type*   24
Critics attack the Byzantine Text   25
The Authorised Version   27
Endnotes   28

THE LORD GAVE THE WORD

A Study in the History of the Biblical Text

—— Malcolm H. Watts ——

The Bible is the eternal Word of God. It has been given by God to man that it might be the absolute, supreme, authoritative, infallible, and unchangeable standard for faith and practice. In this article we shall trace the history of the Bible from its origin in divine self-revelation, through its embodiment in written form by supernatural inspiration, to its accurate transmission to this present age by providential preservation. It is our firm belief that, although the storms of criticism continue to rage against God's Word, the humble believer's confidence in it is justifiable and substantiated. This sacred volume is – and always will be – the Book of God.

The Old Testament

The greater part of the Old Testament was written in Hebrew, sometimes called "the language of Canaan" (Isaiah 19:18) or "the Jews' language" (Isaiah 36:11). It probably developed from the old Hebrew spoken by Abraham in Ur of the Chaldees (Genesis 14:13) and a number of scholars believe that this old Hebrew predated Abraham and that it was the "one language" and "one speech" of pre-Babel times (Genesis 11:1). In other words, they believe it was the original language of man.

THE FIRST LANGUAGE

Supporting evidence for this view is quite substantial. *First of all*, in Hebrew the names of animals express very accurately their nature and characteristics – more so, indeed, than in any other ancient language. This would tie in with the fact that Adam, soon after his creation, gave names to the animals by observing the peculiar qualities and characteristics of each species (Genesis 2:19-20). *Second*, proper names, like Adam, Eve, and Cain, have significant meanings in

Hebrew, some of which are actually assigned to them in the Old Testament Scriptures (Genesis 2:23; 3:20; 4:1). *Third*, the names of various ancient nations appear to be of Hebrew origin, being derived from the sons and grandsons of Shem, Ham and Japheth: as, for example, the Assyrians from Ashur; the Elamites from Elam; and the Aramaeans from Aram.

An argument *can* therefore be made for some form of Hebrew having been the first language spoken and heard in this world; but be that as it may, it is an indisputable fact that practically the whole of the Old Testament is written in Hebrew. The only exceptions are in Aramaic (a close, cognate language to Hebrew) which did, in fact, supersede Hebrew at the time of the captivity. These exceptions are two parts of the book of Ezra (4:8-6:18; 7:12-26), accounted for by Aramaic being the official language of the Persian Empire; a verse in Jeremiah (10:11), where there is a quotation of an Aramaic proverb; and quite a large section of the book of Daniel (2:4 to 7:28), where Aramaic is used, probably because the entire section deals with the nations of the world.

Writing materials

Now on what were the ancient Scriptures written? Originally, the Old Testament Scriptures appear to have been written on papyrus. This was made from reeds which grew on the banks of the Nile River. The reeds were cut into strips and placed line upon line at right angles: then, they were beaten, pressed, and polished to form a kind of primitive paper. We know that papyrus was used in Egypt long ago, certainly in the time of Moses, and it is therefore likely that the first documents of the Old Testament were written on this material. If not, they would have been written on animal skins which were being used around 2,000 BC. Skins came to be preferred because they lasted longer and proved not to be so brittle: hence, they preserved the text more perfectly.

Revelation

We know that God is the greatest of beings. Scripture says, "Canst thou by searching find out God? canst thou find out the Almighty unto perfection?" (Job 11:7). And the answer assumed is, of course, No. We cannot with all our ingenuity discover the infinite God. He is far, far above our human comprehension. Does this mean, then, that we have no hope of knowing Him? Thankfully, it does not mean that. Although we cannot – even with intense investigation – discover God, He *is* able to make Himself known to us. As the source of all truth, He can teach us about His own wonderful Being; and therefore, as the Psalmist says, "In thy light shall we see light" (Psalm 36:9). This brings us, quite naturally, to the doctrine of revelation.

A concise, but accurate, definition of revelation comes from the pen of Dr. James Bannerman. He wrote: "Revelation, as a divine act, is the presentation of objective truth to a man in a supernatural manner by God. Revelation, as the effect of that act, is the objective truth so presented".[1]

Now revelation is of two kinds. First of all, there is *general revelation*. This comes partly from outside us, from the world round about us. In the works of creation and providence, God shows something of His divinity and perfection. "For the invisible things of him from the creation of the world are clearly seen, being understood by the things that are made, *even* His eternal power and Godhead" (Romans 1:20; cf. Psalm 19:1; Acts 14:27). Looking at the various parts of this visible universe, we are compelled to think, with reverential awe, of the divine Architect and Maker. Further general revelation comes from inside us. Made in the image of God, we have some natural sense of God, immortality, and the difference between right and wrong. We are, as Paul says, a law unto ourselves because "the work of the law" is written in our "hearts", our "conscience also bearing witness" (Romans 2:14,15).

Such revelation is said to be general: not only because it is generally made throughout the world, but also because it deals only with general things. It says nothing about specifics, like reconciliation with God, the forgiveness of sins, or the way to heaven.

However, in His wonderful mercy, God has been pleased to grant *special revelation*. This, too, is both external and internal. External special revelation came through "theophanies" as God actually appeared to men and also through "voices", as God spoke to them. "The LORD appeared unto Abram, and said, Unto thy seed will I give this land…" (Genesis 12:7; cf. 3:8-19). Internal special revelation came to chosen men through visions, dreams, and burdens. As God Himself once said, "If there be a prophet among you, *I* the LORD will make myself known unto him in a vision, *and* will speak unto him in a dream" (Numbers 12:6). "Burdens" were heavy messages laid upon the mind and heart. Hence, we read: "The burden of the word of the LORD to Israel by Malachi" (Malachi 1:1). Special revelation meets the deepest needs of men's hearts. It answers the question which is as old as man's soul – "How should man be just with God?" (Job 9:2).

Through general and special revelation (which climaxed, of course, in the Incarnation), God has graciously given to us a divine self-disclosure and made known the way of His salvation.

TWIN DOCTRINE

There is a twin doctrine which we now need to consider: inspiration, which Professor Louis Gaussen once defined as "that inexplicable power which the Divine Spirit put forth of old on the authors of holy Scripture, in order to their guidance even in the employment of the words they used, and to preserve them alike from all error and from all omission".[2]

Inspiration, then, is the *process* by which God exerts a supernatural influence upon certain men, enabling them accurately and infallibly to record whatever has been revealed. "Holy men of God", we read, "spake *as they were* moved by the Holy Ghost" (2 Peter 1:21). The *result* of the process is the written Word of God, "the scripture of truth" (Daniel 10:21). The apostle's classic statement immediately comes to mind: "All scripture *is* given by inspiration of God" (2 Timothy 3:16).

Inspired Scripture is God's book of revelation. As a result of revelation and inspiration, we are able to hold the Bible in our hands and know that we have in our possession the written Word of God.

WRITTEN

The first recorded example of such writing is found in Exodus 17:14 where, soon after the war with the Amalekites, the Lord said to Moses: "Write this *for* a memorial in a book…" Again, in Exodus 24:4, we read how "Moses wrote all the words of the LORD". And yet again, in Exodus 34:27, the Lord said to him, "Write thou these words…" And so we could proceed. There are many other passages showing that Moses wrote more, much more, even the whole of the Pentateuch, i.e., the first five books of the Bible (e.g., Deuteronomy 31:9,24-26; Numbers 33:1,2).

THE ORIGINALS

Once written, the inspired originals, or "autographs" (as they are called), were most carefully preserved. Moses' scroll, for example, was committed to the priests who deposited it near the sacred ark. We read in Deuteronomy 31:25,26 that "Moses commanded the Levites, which bare the ark of the covenant of the LORD, saying, Take this book of the law [the book which he had written] and put it in [or, by] the side of the ark of the covenant of the LORD your God, that it may be there for a witness against thee" (cf. Joshua 1:8; 1 Kings 2:3; Nehemiah 8:1).

After Moses came Joshua, the author of the book which bears his name; and towards the end of his life, according to Joshua 24:26, he did exactly as Moses had once done. Having made an addition to Moses' scroll, he had that scroll replaced in the sanctuary. "And Joshua wrote these words in the book of the law of God, and took a great stone, and set it up there under an oak, that *was* by the sanctuary of the LORD".

It was not long before there was a further addition, this time by Samuel, who "told the people the manner of the kingdom, and wrote *it* in a book, and laid *it* up before the LORD" (i.e., in God's presence, in the holiest apartment and by the ark of the covenant; 1 Samuel 10:25).

THE TEMPLE

When the tabernacle was changed for the temple, these precious originals appear to have been transferred to the more permanent building. There may be a reference to them in 2 Kings 22:8, where Hilkiah, the high priest, is recorded as saying, "I have found the book of the law in the house of the LORD". Some scholars have suggested that this "book of the law" was Moses' original copy, hidden by the priests during the wicked reigns of Manasseh and Amon and only now discovered and brought to the king's attention.[3] In 2 Chronicles 34:14, it is called "a book of the law of the LORD given by Moses". A more literal translation would be "the book of the law of the LORD *by the hand of Moses*".

SIGNIFICANCE OF THE ARK

Dr. W. H. Green points out that keeping these documents in this holy place was "in accordance with the usage of the principal nations of antiquity". He alludes to the fact that "the Romans, Greeks, Phoenicians, Babylonians, and Egyptians had their sacred writings, which were jealously preserved in their temples, and entrusted to the care of officials specially designated for the purpose".[4]

There were, however, more important reasons why the scrolls were laid up in this place:

The ark was enshrined in the divine sanctuary; and writings placed at the side of the ark were therefore *peculiarly associated with God*. He is indeed the author of the Scriptures. What He has said and what the Scriptures say are one and the same thing (Romans 9:17; Galatians 3:2). Here, then, is God's written Word and, as a whole, these inspired books may be called "the oracles of God" (Romans 3:2; cf. Acts 7:38).

Pious Israelites understood the ark to be the throne of God (Exodus 25:22; Psalm 80:1). The fact that these writings were placed by the ark suggested that they were *divinely authoritative*. Scripture possesses tremendous authority. It demands of men unhesitating faith in its teachings and unfaltering obedience to its precepts. Every soul of man must bow to it. "For he established a testimony in Jacob, and appointed a law in Israel, which he commanded our fathers, that they should make them known to their children…" (Psalm 78:5).

Furthermore, since these Scriptures were placed near the ark, in the heart of the tabernacle or temple, they were separated from all common books. They were manifestly declared to be *holy*. Certainly, God's written Word is pure and sublime. It is truth, without any mixture of error. "The words of the LORD *are* pure words: *as* silver tried in a furnace of earth, purified seven times" (Psalm 12:6). The inspired writings should always be revered as "the holy scriptures" (2 Timothy 3:15).

The ark, of course, had its mercy-seat whereon sacrificial blood was sprinkled (Exodus 25:21); and the books were placed nearby, intimating perhaps that they explained the doctrine of atonement and set forth *the only way of approach to God*. "Thus it is written, and thus it behoved Christ to suffer, and to rise from the dead the third day: and that repentance and remission of sins should be preached in his name…" (Luke 24:46,47).

One final thought: the scrolls would have been under the wings of the Cherubim (Exodus 25:18-20), an indication of their being divinely *safeguarded and preserved*. Although often denied today, the doctrine of the preservation of Scripture is to be believed and boldly declared. "The Old Testament in Hebrew…and the New Testament in Greek…being immediately inspired by God, and by His singular care and providence kept pure in all ages, are therefore authentical" (The Westminster Confession of Faith, Chap. 1; Sect. 8). Our Lord Himself said: "Till heaven and earth pass, one jot or one tittle shall in no wise pass from the law, till all be fulfilled" (Matthew 5:18; cf. Psalm 119:152; Isaiah 40:8).

ONE BOOK

God continued to inspire men until there was a wonderful collection of books (1 Chronicles 29:29; 2 Chronicles 9:29, 12:15; Isaiah 30:8; Jeremiah 36:1,2). The earliest of Moses' writings would be dated about 1450 BC, while Malachi's writing would have been finished somewhere around 450 BC. So it was for approximately 1,000 years that God graciously communicated with men and, by the supernatural influence of His Spirit, caused His communications to be written down, free of all error in both fact and doctrine. These writings were then wonderfully preserved. It only remains for us to observe here that, from the beginning, this collection was regarded as essentially one book, called "the book of the LORD" (Isaiah 34:16).

COPIES

The first time copying is mentioned is with respect to the Ten Commandments, originally written of course on tablets of stone by the finger of God. Those first tablets having been broken, the Lord commanded Moses to chisel out new tablets and the Lord wrote on them the same words. It was then that God laid down the rule for copying: the copy must be "according to the first writing" (Deuteronomy 10:4). And we have solid grounds for believing that this rule was strictly enforced. When Jeremiah's written message was destroyed by King Jehoiakim, God told the prophet to make another copy but, in doing so, he stipulated that it had to be an exact copy. "Take thee again another roll", he said, "and write in it all the former words that were in the first roll" (Jeremiah 36:28). Accordingly, Baruch (Jeremiah's scribe) rewrote, under the prophet's dictation, all the words which had been written on the former scroll (36:32 – the second scroll was therefore an accurate copy of the first, even though on this occasion Baruch added further material from Jeremiah's inspired ministry).

So copies were made, not only of the Ten Commandments but also of other parts of Scripture. A copy of the book of Deuteronomy, or perhaps even the whole Pentateuch, was to be in the hands of every king of Israel. "He shall write him a copy of this law in a book out of *that which is* before the priests the Levites: and it shall be with him and he shall read therein all the days of his life" (Deuteronomy 17:18; cf. 2 Chronicles 23:11). The originals, of course, were in the charge of "the priests the Levites"; and when it says, "he shall write him a copy", it probably does not mean that he himself should do this but that he should arrange for someone to do it for him (cf. 1 Samuel 1:3; 13:9; 1 Kings 8:62; John 19:19, where certain men are said to do what, in the event, was almost certainly done by others).

In order to function properly, judges would have needed access to the various laws of Moses (2 Chronicles 19:10), as would the priests, especially those sent with certain Levites to teach in the cities of Judah (2 Chronicles 17:7-9). In the latter case, it is specifically said that "they taught in Judah, and *had* the book of the law of the LORD with them" (v 9). We are not to suppose that only officials possessed copies of the Scriptures. There is evidence to suggest that believers generally had access to biblical books (Psalm 1:4, Psalm 119).

THE WORK OF SCRIBES

Originals, as we have already observed, are called "autographs". Copies are known as "apographs". It is clear that great care was taken in copying the Scriptures. At first, the priests were responsible for this (Deuteronomy 17:18) but later scribes (Hebrew: *sopherim*, from *saphar*, to write) assumed this role, as the language of Jeremiah, the prophet, indicates: "How do ye say,…the law of the LORD *is* with us? Lo, certainly in vain made he *it*; the pen of scribes is in vain" (Jeremiah 8:8). Those designated as scribes originally had many and various responsibilities. However, as time went on, they tended to concentrate on the work of transcription: and hence a man like Ezra came to be called "a scribe of the words of the commandments of the LORD, and of his statutes to Israel" (Ezra 7:11).

Understandably, the demand for copies of the Scriptures became very great. The scribes therefore formed themselves into "families" or "guilds", combining their efforts to ensure the best possible results (1 Chronicles 2:55). Their expertise in this field, together with their profound reverence for Holy Scripture, meant the production of really excellent copies. In fact, only the scrolls which proceeded from this class of scribes were relied upon.

It is worthy of note just here that, in the purpose and providence of God, the Jews took greater care of their sacred writings than any other people in the ancient world.

Such accuracy was achieved that the scribes' copies could be cited as the very Word of God and therefore divinely authoritative. In 1 Kings 2:3, David commands Solomon, his son: "Keep the charge of the LORD thy God, to walk in his ways, to keep his statutes, and his commandments, and his judgments, and his testimonies, as it is written in the law of Moses". Now King Solomon would only have had access to a copy, such as is mentioned in Deuteronomy 17:18,19; but observe how this copy is described as what is "written in the law of Moses". Such painstaking care had taken over the copying that the resultant manuscript retained the authority of the original. It was the Word of God and it could be cited as such.

LOSS OF THE ORIGINALS

Jerusalem fell to the Babylonians in 586 BC. The city suffered dreadful damage and the great temple built by Solomon was completely destroyed (2 Chronicles 36:17-19). Although not mentioned in the history, it is almost certain that the original writings perished along with the city. However, all was not lost. By that time numerous copies had been made and some of these were taken into the land of captivity; for we find Daniel quoting from what must have been a copy of Moses' Law (Daniel 9:11) and also making mention of Jeremiah's prophecy, a copy of which must also have been in his possession (9:2).

In 537 BC, the Jews began to return from their captivity and we know that Ezra re-established worship in Jerusalem "as it is written in the book of Moses" (Ezra 6:18). This suggests that they still had copies of the Scriptures and that they were able to consult them when arranging worship for the second temple. According to Nehemiah 8:1, the people actually requested Ezra to bring "the book of the law of Moses, which the LORD had commanded to Israel". This was not the original – only a copy – yet it is significantly described as "the law of Moses". We conclude from such Scriptures that God had wonderfully preserved His Word.

THE GREAT SYNAGOGUE

The history of the Old Testament ends rather abruptly with the return from captivity; but, according to the later books, Ezra appears to have assumed presidency of a body of learned and wise men (Nehemiah 8:4,7,13; cf. Ezra 7:6,11,22). Jewish tradition informs us that, after the Jews returned, Ezra called into being the Great Synagogue with a view to re-organizing the religious life of the nation. This council – for that is what it really was – consisted of 120 members and came to include the prophets Haggai, Zechariah and Malachi. The "Men of the Great Synagogue" collected together all copies of Holy Scripture which they could find. These, they subjected to detailed examination and comparison. Many minor errors, inadvertently made, were now corrected. These errors were such as the omission of a letter, a word, or perhaps even a line. That they had crept into some manuscripts is not at all surprising when we remember that there are at least eight pairs of Hebrew letters which are similar, even to the point of being nearly identical. The most conscientious of scribes was not beyond making a small mistake. Eventually, however, the copies underwent correction and if any were found particularly faulty, they were buried in a "genizah", a holy place near to a Jewish synagogue. As a result of the Great Synagogue's work, the Second Temple appears to have been supplied with a text very similar to the later, received Hebrew text.[5]

By the time our Lord came on the scene, many reliable copies were available. The Lord Jesus constantly appealed to the sacred Scriptures. He read from them in the synagogues (Luke 4:16); He quoted from them in His public ministry (Matthew 19:3-5; 21:16,42); and He exhorted His hearers to read them for themselves (John 5:39). There can be no doubt that He regarded the extant copies as the very Word of God. Although He corrected Pharisaical interpretations and glosses, *never once did He call into question the integrity of the Hebrew text*. He was able to say, "It is written" (Matthew 4:4,7,10) and, again, "the scripture cannot be broken" (John 10:35). The same applies, of course, to the Apostles (Acts 1:16, 4:25, 28:25; Hebrews 1:1,6,7; etc.).

It might be argued that this proves too much, insofar as the Septuagint (LXX: the Greek translation of the Old Testament made by Alexandrian Jews around 250 BC) is also constantly quoted in the New Testament, without ever once being called into question. On the same premise, therefore, could this not be said to indicate endorsement of the Septuagint as an inspired and accurate text? No, there is a serious flaw in such reasoning. The fact is that there are a number of places in the New Testament where the Septuagint version appears to have been deliberately rejected (e.g., Matthew 2:15, where the LXX reads: "Out of Egypt I called his children"; Romans 10:15, where the LXX reads, "I am present as a season of beauty upon the mountains, as the feet of one preaching glad tidings of peace, as one preaching good news". See also: Romans 11:4; 1 Peter 4:8).

While some New Testament quotations show preference for the Septuagint rendering, the variation in these cases will be found to be very slight, and not at all in sense (e.g., Matthew 15:8,9 - Hebrew: "...their heart they have removed far from me, and their fearing of me has become a precept of men, a thing taught"; Acts 13:34 - Hebrew: "I will give you the sure mercies of David", but the New Testament Greek text actually quotes the Septuagint here, as in the *margin* of our Authorised Version: "[I will give] to you...the holy things of David, the sure things").

Furthermore, the purpose behind quoting the Septuagint Version is often to bring out more clearly the intended meaning of the original (See: Romans 10:18, where the rendering "sound" is preferred to the Hebrew "line", a somewhat obscure expression, although as a "string" of a musical instrument, it clearly means much the same thing).

"We do not find", comments Dr. Roger Nicole, "any example of a New Testament deduction or application logically inferred from the Septuagint and which cannot be maintained on the basis of the Hebrew text". He concludes: "The use of the LXX in quoting does not indicate that the New Testament writers have thought of this version as inspired in itself... Yet their willingness to make use of the LXX, in spite of its occasional defects, teaches the important lesson that the basic message God purposed to deliver can be conveyed even through a translation, and that appeal can be made to a version insofar as it agrees with the original".[6]

To return to our earlier point: the endorsement given by our Lord and His apostles to the first-century Hebrew text shows that text to have been both accurate and reliable.

THE FAMOUS MASSORETES

As we have seen, God raised up scribes, or sopherim, to produce a remarkably pure text. It fell to others to continue their work and take the necessary steps for the text's preservation. These were the Massoretes, a name derived from the Hebrew word "Massorah" which means "tradition". They were families of Jewish scholars and textual critics who eventually opened academies, one at Tiberias (on the coast of the sea of Galilee) and another in Babylon (in the East). No-one knows exactly when the Massoretes first appeared. Some believe they can be traced back to the first century AD. Others date their beginnings later, somewhere around 500 AD. Whichever is correct, the Massoretes' achievement is what really matters.

Jerusalem had been destroyed in AD 70. As a result, the Jews were scattered throughout the various countries of the Roman Empire. The Massoretes knew that these dispersed Jews and their succeeding generations would require copies of the Holy Scriptures and they believed that certain things could be done to ensure the preservation of the pure Hebrew text. With this in mind, they collected vital information about the text and laid down detailed rules for the proper copying of it.

They introduced vowel-points (Hebrew has no vowels), fixed accents (to ensure correct pronunciation), explained the meaning of words (where ambiguity existed), supplied marginal readings (to remove obscurity), and marked intended pauses (which often affect the meaning). So meticulous were they in their studies that they even counted the verses, words, and letters of the Old Testament, noting for example, that Aleph occurs 42,377 times; Beth, 38,218 times; Gimel, 29,537 times; and so on.

Copyists had to follow the Talmud's strict rules, which included the following: only the skins of clean animals were to be used; each skin must contain the same number of columns; there were to be no less than forty-eight and no more than sixty lines; black ink was to be prepared according to a particular recipe; no word or letter was to be written from memory; if so much as a letter was omitted, or wrongly inserted, or even if one letter touched another, the sheet had to be destroyed; three mistakes on a page meant the whole manuscript was condemned; and revision of the copy had to take place within 30 days, for otherwise it had to be rejected. A manuscript surviving this process could hardly be anything but amazingly accurate.

A Massoretic Text

The Massoretes' purpose was to preserve the Old Testament from every kind of alteration; and it was to secure that objective that they made their collection of detailed notes (the Massorah). The Jews called their finished work "The Fence of the Law". As a result of their labours, we possess today a standard and traditional text.

The text from which our Authorised Version was translated is called the Ben Chayyim Text (after Jacob ben Chayyim, under whose editorship it was printed in 1524-5) and it is similar to the Text of Ben Asher (who lived in the tenth century at Tiberias, in Palestine, and who, along with members of his family, established an accurate edition of the Massoretic Text). This is a faithful and dependable text.

Through God's special providence, we are able confidently to say that in *the Hebrew Massoretic text* we have a text which is very close to the Hebrew Original.

OLD TESTAMENT SUMMARY

Summing up, then, what were the means God used to ensure the preservation of His Word?

The first was the Jew's profound reverence for the Holy Scriptures. A Jew would literally tremble before the written Word. According to Philo and Josephus, they would suffer any torments, and even death itself, rather than change anything in the Holy Scriptures. God used this reverence for the text to prevent it from being falsified and corrupted.

Second, there were the solemn commands of the Scriptures, such as Deuteronomy 4:2: "Ye shall not add unto the word which I command you, neither shall ye diminish *ought* from it". These commands, issued with divine authority, instilled genuine fear into men's hearts.

Third, these scrolls were laid up in the Holy of Holies. There being no more sacred spot on earth, it placed them beyond the reach of interfering hands.

Fourth, the sheer professionalism of the scribes and Massoretes secured and preserved a pure text. They were great scholars, skilled in the divine law and revered as interpreters of the Holy Scriptures.

Fifth, there was the oversight of prophets. Throughout the Old Testament period, prophets exercised a unique ministry and they were well able to superintend the copying work. Any error in transcription would have been quickly detected by them.

Sixth, the Jews constantly repeated their Scriptures, as Deuteronomy 6:7 clearly shows: "Thou shalt teach them diligently unto thy children, and shalt talk of them when thou sittest in thine house, and when thou walkest by the way, and when thou liest down, and when thou risest up". These repetitions created such familiarity with the text that if so much as a word had been altered, it would have been immediately noticed and, without doubt, strong and even vehement protest would have been made.

Seventh, Christ and His apostles confirmed the Scriptures as they were received in their times. The standard text used by them is the very same as we use today. Their unhesitating citation of it as God's Word is an indisputable seal of its authenticity and reliability.

These and other considerations lead us to believe that God has wonderfully preserved the Old Testament text. When the Old Testament is read, according to the Massoretic text, we can believe that we are reading and hearing the Word of God. Interesting as they may be, it is not for us to accept *peculiar renderings* from the Dead Sea Scrolls, from the Latin version, or from any other source.

God has *preserved* His Word. This is not to be understood as meaning that, throughout history, God has performed repeated miracles, nor that He has "inspired" the various rabbis and scribes who worked on the text. We concede that the autographs have long since perished and that some errors have crept into the copies now available to us. Hence there is need for textual criticism. The doctrine of "providential preservation" requires careful definition. What exactly do we mean by it? Here, I would quote the words of Professor John H. Skilton: "God who gave the Scriptures, who works all things after the counsel of his will, has exercised a remarkable care over his Word, has preserved it in all ages in a state of essential purity, and has enabled it to accomplish the purpose for which he gave it".[7]

The Hebrew text, then, was originally given by Moses and the prophets; it was faithfully copied by the scribes, standardized by Ezra along with the Men of the Great Synagogue, endorsed by our Lord and His apostles, and edited with meticulous care by the Massoretes. Orthodoxy requires that we boldly affirm our faith in the Old Testament as translated from the Hebrew Massoretic text.

The New Testament

The Lord Jesus Christ ascribed inspired authority to the Old Testament Scriptures (Matthew 5:18; 15:3; Mark 12:36; John 10:35). He also promised that, after His return to heaven, He would send the Spirit of God to communicate further truth to His chosen servants and enable them to record it. This would provide the Christian Church with an infallible guide. "The Comforter", He said, "*which is* the Holy Ghost, whom the Father will send in my name, he shall teach you all things, and bring all things to your remembrance, whatsoever I have said unto you" (John 14:26; cf. 16:12,13).

At first, there was only oral teaching. It soon became apparent, however, that Christian truth needed to be committed to writing. For one thing, the apostles (the witnesses of our Lord in the days of His flesh) were beginning to travel to distant lands and before long they would all be removed by death (2 Timothy 4:6; 2 Peter 1:14); for another, the ever increasing number of new converts and churches were in need of regular, detailed, and comprehensive instruction (Luke 1:3,4; Acts 1:1); and for yet another, spurious and heretical writings, even then in circulation, were causing serious doctrinal confusion (2 Thessalonians 2:1,2; 3:17).

The Holy Spirit, anticipating all this, exerted His supernatural influence on certain chosen men so that they wrote down what was infallible and inerrant. Thus, at the end of his Gospel, John describes himself as "the disciple which testifieth of these things, and wrote these things", and adds, "we know that his testimony is true" (John 21:24,25; cf. 1 Corinthians 14:37; Galatians 1:20; Philippians 3:1; 1 John 1:4; etc.).

CHRISTIAN TRUTH WRITTEN DOWN

Thus the New Testament Scriptures came into being. At first, they were written in Greek which was the common language of the Roman Empire at the time when Christianity began. The writing was committed to specially prepared materials: "papyrus" (a paper-like substance, made from the pith of the papyrus plant) and, later on, "parchment" (animal skin, called "vellum" when particularly fine in quality). In outward form, the documents would have looked like scrolls (if papyrus) and books (if parchment or vellum). The technical name for the latter is codices (the singular of which is codex).

As for the pens used, they would have been reed or quill-pens (made from stalks or feathers) and the ink would almost certainly have been black and carbon-based (prepared with soot and mixed with gum). Later, in about the fifth century, a red metallic ink (prepared from gall-apples) was used, but this appears only to have been used for emphasis.

There are, of course, references in the New Testament to "writing", "paper (papyrus) and ink", and also to "books" and "parchments" (i.e. parchments of prepared skins). See: 2 Timothy 4:13; 2 Corinthians 3:3; 2 John 12; and 3 John 13. An interesting question now arises: What happened to these original documents?

THE DIVINE ORIGINALS

Immediately recognized by the early Christians as divinely authoritative (1 Corinthians 14:37), these texts were first read by those to whom they were sent, whether individuals or churches, and then they were circulated so that as many as possible could benefit from the apostles' teachings (1 Thessalonians 5:27; Revelation 1:3; Colossians 4:16; 2 Peter 3:15,16). Sadly, these originals (or "autographs") could not have survived long, partly because they tended to become brittle and constant use soon caused them to disintegrate, and partly because they were exposed to hazards of both accident and persecution.

There may possibly be a reference to the originals in a treatise dated about 200 AD. Tertullian, one of the Early Church Fathers, was responsible for a treatise entitled "The Prescription against Heretics" and, in the thirty-sixth chapter, he wrote: "Come now, you who would indulge a better curiosity,…run over the apostolic churches…in which their own *authentic* writings are read… Achaia is very near you, (in which) you find Corinth. Since you are not far from Macedonia, you have Philippi; (and there too) you have the Thessalonians. Since you are able to cross to Asia, you get Ephesus. Since, moreover, you are close upon Italy, you have Rome, from which there comes even into our own hands the very authority (of apostles themselves)".[8]

Although denied by some scholars, it is affirmed by others that the reference here is to the Greek originals. Tertullian, it is said, is urging his readers to visit those places where the originals are being kept and thus to see for themselves the divine and sacred writings of the New Testament.[9]

Accurate copying

Be that as it may, the apostles' own manuscripts would almost certainly not have lasted much beyond the year 200 AD. Yet our Lord had intimated that the Christian Scriptures would be preserved. "Heaven and earth shall pass away", He said, "but my words shall not pass away" (Matthew 24:35; cf. 28:20; Mark 8:38; 1 Peter 1:23-25). Their preservation was ensured, of course, by faithful and conscientious copying.

Even in apostolic times, copies of New Testament books were in the possession both of individuals and of churches. Peter, at any rate, was familiar with Paul's epistle to the Christians living in Asia Minor (Galatians, Ephesians, or Colossians) and, indeed, he intimates quite clearly that he was acquainted with "all [Paul's] epistles" (2 Peter 3:15,16). The Colossian church was told that Paul's letter to them was not to be regarded in any sense as their peculiar property, but it – almost certainly a copy – was to be "read also in the church of the Laodiceans". The Colossians were further told, "ye likewise read the epistle" – again, probably a copy – "from Laodicea" (probably Ephesians; Colossians 4:16). Before long, there were collections of these books. Christian churches needed whole sets for reading in public worship.

This is indirectly confirmed by the writings of the Apostolic Fathers in the second century. For brevity's sake, reference can be made to only one of them: Polycarp, a disciple of the apostle John. Writing to the Philippians, he quotes extensively from the Gospels and the Epistles and then expresses his confidence that the Philippians themselves are "well versed in the Sacred Scriptures".[10] By this time, copies had certainly been made and the evidence suggests that they were widely circulated.

The first copies may have been made by the apostles themselves. Paul, in his Roman prison, requested that he be brought "books, *but* especially the parchments" (2 Timothy 4:13). J.P. Lilley suggests that "the 'parchments' may have been *copies or portions* of the Scriptures or even *of his own letters* to the Churches".[11] It is also supposed – and with some probability – that John prepared seven copies of his "Revelation" and sent one to each of the seven churches of Asia Minor (Revelation 1:4-6; 2:1,8,18, etc).[12]

If the apostles themselves were not always responsible for copying, then it is likely that the work was often done by their secretaries. We know for certain that such were sometimes employed to write books or letters (Romans 16:22; 1 Peter 5:12). Why should they not be seconded to the work of copying?

"Scribes", originally equivalent to "secretaries" (Ezra 4:8; Esther 3:12; Jeremiah 8:8), had been promised to the Christian Church. "Behold," said our Lord, "I send unto you prophets, and wise men, and scribes…"(Matthew 23:34; cf. 13:52). We may suppose that such were among Paul's assistants. Indeed, the apostle makes reference to "Zenas the lawyer and Apollos" (Titus 3:13).

The copyists transcribed these documents with scrupulous care. How can we be sure about this? *First of all*, these New Testament books were invested with the same sanctity as were the Old Testament Scriptures (I Timothy 5:18 which cites Luke 10:7, along with Deuteronomy 25:4, as "scripture"; and 2 Peter 3:16 which places Paul's epistles in the same category as "the other scriptures"). *Second*, nearly all the early copyists would have been hired or converted Jewish scribes whose reverence for God's written Word compelled them to study perfect accuracy in transcription (Jeremiah 36:28; cf. Deuteronomy 10:4). *Third*, the writings themselves, claiming to be the inspired and authoritative Word of God, issued most severe prohibitions against any kind of tampering with the holy text (1 Corinthians 2:13; 2 Corinthians 2:17; Revelation 22:18,19). *Fourth*, knowing that the apostles were still alive and active, the early copyists would have been all the more careful to produce manuscripts of first-class quality. *Fifth*, and finally, if at first the task of making copies was committed to the apostles' fellow-workers who were known as "evangelists" (and according to Eusebius it was their responsibility to "give [new converts] the book of the divine Gospels"),[13] it should be remembered that these men received the miraculous gifts of the Holy Spirit and were therefore peculiarly equipped to preserve the inspired text (2 Timothy 1:6, 4:5).

Furthermore, there is a divine factor which must not be overlooked. In His superintending and gracious providence, God evidently ensured that the authentic text of the New Testament was transmitted to future generations.

TEXTUAL VARIANTS

Notwithstanding all this, errors did appear in some copies and, as more copies were made, there began to appear a number of variant readings. These are usually classified as (1) *unintentional* changes, and (2) *intentional* changes. The unintentional kind include misspelt words, confusion of letters, changes in the word-order, the use of synonyms or verbal equivalents, and the omission or repetition of letters, words, lines, and even sections. By far the largest number of variants are due to slips like these on the part of the scribes.

There are, however, intentional changes, by which we mean deliberate tampering with the sacred text, usually in the interests of a particular theology or doctrine. Dionysius, a minister at Corinth, in a letter dated about AD 168-170, deplores the fact that his own letters have been altered, and then adds: "It is not marvellous, therefore, if some have set themselves to tamper with the Dominical Scriptures".[14] An unknown author (thought by some to be Hippolytus, but by others, Gaius) writes somewhere around AD 230: "They (the heretics) laid hands fearlessly on the divine Scriptures, saying that they had corrected them".[15] Who were the heretics who dared to do such a thing?

Some are practically unknown, as Asclepiades, Theodotus, Hermophilus, and Apollonides, but others were well-known as, for example, some of the early Gnostics (who taught salvation through a secret knowledge): Basilides, Valentinus, and of course Marcion, who accepted as canon only his mutilated editions of Luke's Gospel and ten of the Pauline epistles. "Marcion expressly and openly used the knife, not the pen, since he made such an excision of the Scriptures as suited his own subject-matter".[16]

Reproducing the Authentic New Testament Text

Orthodox teachers were fully aware of these wicked alterations, exposing them both in their teachings and in their writings. As a result, manuscripts considered faulty were not generally used for copying purposes. Only those which faithfully preserved the original became the standard documents from which multiplied copies were made.

Do we have any evidence, however, for believing that this is indeed what happened?

Early Christian leaders certainly claimed ability to evaluate the various manuscripts and decide which were the best and most accurate. For example, Irenaeus in his great work "Against Heresies" refers to "the most approved and ancient copies".[17] The kind of criteria used to ascertain a faithful text would be such as the following:

1. *The identity of the copyist.* If he was an ordinary Christian man, his copy would probably contain a number of mistakes. If, on the other hand, he was known to be an apostolic assistant or professional scribe, a very high degree of accuracy could be expected.

2. *The nature of the manuscript from which the copy was made.* In earliest times this may have been the inspired original, but later it would certainly have been itself a copy. Now many copies were what we call "private" copies: that is, such as were intended for personal and devotional use. Some, however, were "official" copies from which Christian ministers read and preached in the services of public worship. The latter would always prove far more reliable than the former. Copies made from these would share much of their reliability.

3. *The number of copyings which had already taken place.* A copy of the original or one of the earliest copies of the original would be far more likely to provide a sound text than a copy with a long and rather complicated line of descent. Hence, the oldest copy was not always reckoned the best, for it may have been copied from another of the same period, whereas a later copy may have been copied from a much earlier one, close to the original.

4. *The place where the copy was found.* Churches themselves became the custodians of the pure Word of God (as was the case formerly with local synagogues); and if the copied document had been preserved in a church, one could be reasonably certain that it was a recognized, true and proper transcript.

5. The general quality of the copy. Some copies are manifestly faulty. They are badly written and full of mistakes of the most palpable character. Whoever produced them was either ignorant or careless – or, of course, both. These would neither be regarded nor used as trustworthy witnesses to the authentic New Testament text. The carefully written copies, however, would inspire confidence and, as a result, they would be painstakingly transcribed.

6. The agreement with other existing copies. It would be a mistake to assume that a scribe had only one text before him. In the first two centuries there was a rapid multiplication of copies, so it was possible by comparing copies to detect odd readings and, in the same way, to ascertain what the inspired writers actually wrote. The early Christians were in a far better position to do this than we are. After all, they had access to manuscripts which have long since perished.

7. The close proximity to a well-known Christian centre. A copy made at a distance from where apostles and their immediate successors had regularly ministered would be the most likely to have suffered some serious changes or alterations; but a copy made in an area of early church activity would very probably be the representative of a pure textual tradition.

Orthodox teachers of the first and second centuries may not always have had access to the best manuscripts but they appear to have known how to identify "the approved and ancient copies". Every attempt was made to utilize their underlying text, with the result that *the overwhelming majority of early Greek manuscripts were in essential agreement.* We may therefore believe that *the text of the majority represented the Original with impressive accuracy.*

THE SURVIVING GREEK MANUSCRIPTS

According to one recent list, the total number of manuscripts of the whole or a part of the New Testament is 5,488.[18] They are placed in the usual categories:

1. *Papyri.*

According to the 1989 statistics, there are 96 of these catalogued. Nearly all are fragmentary, although originally they would have appeared in codex or book form. They have mainly been discovered in Egypt where the climate and sand have helped to preserve them. When referring to these fragments, scholars use the letter 'P' followed by a serial number: P1, P2, P3 and so on.

P52 (the so-called Rylands fragment) is reckoned the oldest. It measures only 2 1/2 by 3 1/2 inches and contains a few verses from the Gospel of John (18:31-33, 37-38). It is dated approximately 125 AD.

Among the most important are P45, P46, and P47. Known as the Chester Beatty Biblical papyri (after Sir Chester Beatty who acquired them in 1930-1), these contain portions from the Gospels, the Pauline Epistles and the book of Revelation. Another important collection is the Bodmer Library collection (acquired by M. Martin Bodmer from 1956 onwards). This includes P66, pages and fragments from a codex of John's Gospel, written around 200 AD; and P72, a third century copy – and therefore possibly the earliest we have – of the Epistles of Peter and Jude.

2. Uncials.

There are 299 known uncials. Written from the beginning of the fourth century on parchment or vellum and in codex or book form, they are all in the uncial script: that is, they are all written in capital letters with no punctuation. The earlier ones are actually designated by capital letters along with serial numbers beginning with a zero (e.g., A-02). Later ones simply have the numbers (e.g., 046).

Among those in the British Museum is Codex Alexandrinus, A-02. This was copied in Egypt in the first half of the fifth century and, when complete, it contained the whole Greek Bible along with one or two apocryphal works. It now contains practically the whole of the Old Testament and most of the New (omitting Matthew 1:1-25:6; John 6:50-8:52; 2 Corinthians 4:13-12:7). The Patriarch of Alexandria presented this manuscript to Charles I in 1627.

Another codex which dates from the fifth century is Codex Bezae, D-05. In 1581, Theodore Beza, successor to John Calvin, presented this manuscript to Cambridge University where it still remains. This codex has both Greek and Latin texts (the left page in the former, the right in the latter) and it contains most of the Gospels and the Book of Acts, together with a few verses from 3 John.

The most famous of the uncials are Codex Sinaiticus, Aleph-01 (Aleph being the first letter of the Hebrew alphabet), and Codex Vaticanus, B-03.

Codex Sinaiticus, dated in the mid- or late-fourth century, contains only a part of the Old Testament but the whole of the Greek New Testament. It is the only complete uncial manuscript of the New Testament extant. This Egyptian codex was written on vellum, with four columns of forty-eight lines on each page, but there are clear indications in the text itself that it has several times been corrected. In the year 1844 Constantine Tischendorf discovered some of its leaves in a waste-paper basket in the library of St. Catherine's monastery on Mount Sinai. He had to wait until 1859, however, before he had sight of the whole New Testament. After obtaining permission, he transferred it to Cairo where he produced a copy of it; and in 1862, through the generosity of Alexander II, the Russian Emperor, he published an edition of the manuscript with an Introduction and Critical Notes.

Codex Vaticanus may also be dated about the middle of the fourth century and, like Aleph, it is written on fine vellum but with three columns to the page, each consisting of forty-two lines. Once a complete Greek Bible, it has long since lost portions of the Old Testament and several large sections of the New Testament. Missing from this uncial are the Pastoral Epistles, Philemon, the conclusion of Hebrews (9:14 to the end), and the whole of the book of Revelation. Various correctors have been at work on the manuscript and, in the tenth century, someone traced over much of the original, fearing, it seems, that its letters might otherwise fade away. Peculiarities in spelling suggest an Alexandrian origin but no-one knows how it came into the Library of the Vatican in Rome. The Library was founded in 1448 by Pope Nicolas V and this manuscript is listed in the earliest catalogue, issued in 1475. Samuel Tregelles tried to consult it in 1845 but he was greatly hindered by its clerical custodians. In 1866, Tischendorf was given permission to study it for forty-two hours and, from his study and notes, an edition of this manuscript – Codex B – was produced in 1867. This was followed by an edition issued by the Papal authorities and prepared by Vercellone and Cozza in 1868; and, then, in 1889-90, a photographic facsimile was made available to scholars.

3. *Minuscules.*

There are 2,812 of these. They are called minuscules because they are written not with capitals but with small letters (called minuscules or cursives). This style of writing had been used for centuries in private documents but it was not until the ninth century that it was used for literary purposes. With the demand for New Testament books ever increasing, this script had the advantages of taking less time to write and of occupying less space on the parchment. For purposes of identification, they are designated by ordinary numbers (1,2,3 and so on).

The minuscules, then, were written from the ninth century onwards; but their later date does not necessarily mean that they are less credible witnesses to the originals. Ninth century manuscripts may have been copied from others of the third century. As Professor Warfield once observed, "It is not the mere number of years that is behind any ms. that measures its distance from the autograph, but the number of copyings".[19]

These minuscules include the following:

MS 1: a codex of the twelfth century, containing the whole of the New Testament, apart from the book of Revelation. MS 4: a twelfth century copy of the four Gospels. MS 12: an eleventh century copy of the Gospels. MS 21: from the tenth century but also containing the Gospels. MS 43: an eleventh century work in two volumes, the first containing the Gospels and the second, the Acts and the Epistles. MS 330: eleventh century, containing the Gospels, Acts, and Epistles. MS 565: a very fine ninth century copy of the Gospels, written in gold letters on purple vellum.

4. *Lectionaries.*

Totalling 2,281, these are texts from as early as the sixth century, containing the Gospels and Epistles (Evangeliaria and Apostoli) appointed to be read in the early Christian churches. Most of them use uncial letters but some are minuscules; and, once again, designation is by numbers but this time prefixed with an '*l*' or with the abbreviation 'Lect' (e.g., *l*59 or Lect. 1280).

These are important manuscripts, not only because some of them are early, but also because they were used for reading in the public services of the Church. *The greatest care would have been taken over these church copies to preserve their original purity*; and *the testimony of a lectionary* would be, in effect, *the testimony of all the churches*. Now, the surviving lectionaries which have been examined are found to agree to an amazing extent. The only reasonable explanation, surely, is that there was *a recognized lectionary text*.

CLASSIFICATION

A great number of Greek manuscripts is therefore available to us, written from as early as the second century. Scholars who have studied them maintain that, while there are variants, certain manuscripts have a great many readings in common which suggests that there are groups or families. The major text-types are as follows: (i) the Byzantine (sometimes called the Traditional, Majority, or Antiochian text); (ii) the Alexandrian (or what some have called Neutral Text); (iii) the Western; and (iv) the Caesarean.

For the purposes of this article, the last two text-types do not require detailed comment. It was B.H. Streeter, in *The Four Gospels* (1924), who first claimed to have found the Caesarean text. He believed that this was the text of Mark's Gospel which Origen quoted after 231 AD, the year in which he came to Caesarea. Modern textual critics, however, doubt whether this can really be called a distinct text-type. They tend rather to think of it as a mere mixture.

As for the Western text-type, identified by B.F. Westcott and F.J.A. Hort, and thought to originate in Western Europe, there would appear to be *some* evidence for its existence. It is represented by Codex Bezae (fifth century), Codex Claromontanus (sixth century), and the Old Latin and Curetonian Syriac translations (third and fifth centuries respectively). It is also quoted by some of the early Church Fathers, such as Irenaeus, Tertullian, and Cyprian. However, this text-type is often radically different from all others. It is marred by a number of omissions, not only of verses but also of whole passages. Its prevailing tendency, however, is to make additions, either by way of paraphrase or by the insertion of additional details. In the Gospels (especially in the latter part of Luke's Gospel) it is shorter, while in the Acts it is a great deal longer (approximately 10% longer). Sir Frederic Kenyon described it as "a type of text characterised by very free departures from the true tradition". Paucity of manuscript support, along with a multitude of distinctive readings, renders this text-type at best questionable, at worst wholly unreliable.

This really leaves us with two major groups of texts: the Byzantine and the Alexandrian.

A. *The Byzantine Text-type*

This text receives its name from the fact that it was early associated with the imperial capital of Constantinople, formerly called Byzantium, and also from the fact that it became the standard text of the Christian Church throughout the Byzantine period, 312-1453 AD (and actually long after that). Prior to its enthronement in the Eastern capital, however, this form of text had been preserved in Antioch, capital of the Roman province of Syria. Christian teachers connected with the church there clearly used it. These include Basil of Caesarea, Gregory of Nyssa, Gregory of Nazianzus (the Cappadocian Fathers), Theodoret of Cyrus, and Chrysostom of Constantinople (who moved from Antioch to become bishop of Constantinople in 398 AD).

The Byzantine text-type has *overwhelming support from the Greek manuscripts*.

In the early papyri there is an impressive number of distinctively Byzantine readings. P45 and P46 of the Chester Beatty Papyri contain such readings, as does P66 of the Bodmer Library collection. Professor H. A. Sturz was able to list *150 Byzantine readings with early papyri support.*[20] This plainly shows that, contrary to the views of earlier textual critics, the Byzantine readings can be traced as far back as the second century.

Among the Uncials, this text is found in the fifth century Codices Alexandrinus (A-02; Byzantine in the Gospels), and Ephraemi (C-01), and in practically all the later ones. It is estimated that approximately 95% of the Uncial manuscripts have a Byzantine type of text. Even more can be claimed for the Minuscules, since nearly all of these are Byzantine in their readings.

The Lectionaries thus far examined also give support to the Byzantine text-type.

☐ *1. Supported by the early Versions*

These were the early translations of the New Testament Scriptures, prepared to help spread the Christian Faith among the peoples of the world. Among the earliest known to us are the Syriac (or Aramaic) and Latin Versions which go back to the mid-second century. The Peshitta, "Queen of Versions", is one of the early Syriac translations and it certainly contains Byzantine readings. This is also true of the Gothic version of the fourth century, said to be translated by Ufilas, bishop of Antioch.

☐ *2. Confirmed by the early Fathers*

Critics who deny the primacy of the Byzantine text, preferring to view it as a fourth century revision, often refer to the fact no Early Church Father before Chrysostom (347-407 AD) appears even to refer to it, let alone quote from it. Now this is simply not true. Painstaking scholarly research has shown that Justin Martyr (100-165 AD), Irenaeus (130-200 AD), Clement of Alexandria (150-215 AD), Tertullian (160-220 AD), Hippolytus (170-236 AD), and even Origen (185-254 AD) quote repeatedly from the Byzantine text. Edward Miller, after classifying the citations in the Greek and Latin Fathers who died before 400 AD, found that their quotations supported the Byzantine text 2,630 times (and other texts only 1,753 times). Furthermore, subjecting thirty important passages to examination, he found 530 testimonies to the Byzantine text (and only 170 in favour of its opponents). This was his conclusion: "The original predominance of the Traditional Text is shewn in the list of the earliest Fathers. Their record proves that in their writings, and so in the Church generally, corruption had made itself felt in the earliest times, but that the pure waters generally prevailed... The tradition is also carried on through the majority of the Fathers who succeeded them. There is no break or interval: the witness is continuous".[21]

The plain fact of the matter is that by the fourth century the Byzantine text was emerging as the authoritative text of the New Testament and for the next twelve hundred years (and more) it held undisputed sway over the whole of Christendom.

☐ 3. *The Printed Greek New Testament*

The Greek New Testament was first printed in 1514, although not published in a separate edition until 1522. This was the work of Francisco Ximenes, Cardinal Primate of Spain, and it formed part of his six-volume Complutensian Polyglot. In his Dedication to Pope Leo X, Ximenes wrote: "For Greek copies indeed we are indebted to your Holiness, who sent us most kindly from the Apostolic Library very ancient codices, both of the Old and New Testament; which have aided us very much in this undertaking". The resultant Greek text appears to be have been of the Byzantine type (and there is no evidence that Ximenes ever followed the Codex Vaticanus [B]).

In 1516, when Desiderius Erasmus, the foremost scholar in Europe, published the first edition of the Greek New Testament, he based it on representative Byzantine manuscripts. Erasmus issued four further editions of his work, in 1519, 1522, 1527, and 1535. Others soon followed in his footsteps: most notably, Robert Estienne (Latinized as Stephanus), the French editor and printer, whose published text in 1546 was practically identical with that of Erasmus. There were three subsequent editions in 1549, 1550, and 1551. Still further editions were edited and published by Theodore Beza between 1565 and 1604. Then, in 1624, Bonaventure and Abraham Elzevir issued their edition. The Preface to the Elzevirs' second edition, published in 1633, contains the words: "Therefore you have a text now received by all, in which we give no alteration or corruption". From this came the now familiar name *"The Received Text"*.

The Byzantine text was *the underlying text of all the great English Protestant Bibles*, including those associated with the names of William Tyndale (1525), Miles Coverdale (1535), John Rogers (1537), and Richard Taverner (1539), as well as those known as The Great Bible (1539), The Geneva Bible (1560), The Bishops' Bi-

A Study in the History of the Biblical Text

ble (1568), and, of course, the Authorized Version (1611); and the Reina in Spanish, the Karoli in Hungarian, the Luther in German, the Olivetan in French, the Statenvertaling in Dutch, the Almeida in Portuguese and the Diodati in Italian.

Summing up here, the arguments in favour of the Byzantine text are as follows:

1. This text-type is *associated with the city of Antioch in Syria*. After Stephen's death, Christians from Jerusalem fled to this city and began to preach the Gospel to the Greeks there (Acts 11:19,20). A strong church came into being, largely through the ministries of Barnabas and Paul (11:22-26), and from this church the apostle started on each of his missionary journeys (Acts 13:1-3, 15:35,36, 18:22,23). Other apostles visited the place, including the apostle Peter (Galatians 2:11,12). It was not long before Antioch became the mother city of Gentile churches and, after the fall of Jerusalem in 70 AD, it became the true undisputed centre of Christianity. A text proceeding from Antioch would be the text approved by the apostles and the early Christian Church.

2. As has already been observed, this text received its name from Constantinople (Byzantium), the capital of the Eastern Empire, because it soon became established there as the standard Greek text. Constantinople was the centre both of the Greek-speaking world and of the Greek-speaking Church, for whereas in the West, Greek had given way to Latin, in the East, it had remained the official and common language. This meant, of course, that *Greek scholars in Constantinople were peculiarly fitted to recognize and reproduce the authentic text.*

3. *During the fourth century when this text became supreme, the Church was blessed with exceptional scholars* such as Methodius (AD 260-312), Athanasius (296-373), Hilary of Poitiers (315-67), Cyril of Jerusalem (315-386), and Gregory of Nazianzen (330-394). These men – and others like them – were involved in formularizing orthodox doctrine and ratifying the canon of the New Testament. They also devoted themselves to the study of the text; and they had an advantage over later critics on account of their access to many early and invaluable manuscripts which long since have perished. The emergence of a predominant text from this period is highly significant. It was obviously considered the genuine, uncorrupted, and authorised text.

4. The Jews were appointed the guardians of the divine revelations imparted to them and, in fulfilment of the trust reposed in them, they carefully preserved the Old Testament text uncorrupted and entire (the Hebrew Massoretic text). As the apostle Paul has observed, "unto them were committed the oracles of God" (Romans 3:2). Now it is reasonable to suppose that *the New Testament Scriptures were committed to professing Christians, or to the professing Christian Church.* The question which naturally arises is: Which text-type, generally speaking, has been recognized and propagated by the Church from earliest times? The answer is: the text-type known as Byzantine.

The Lord gave the Word

5. The fact is that *approximately 90% of the Greek manuscripts represent the Byzantine text-type.* Although these manuscripts are not as early as some critics would have liked, they are so numerous that we must assume that there were literally hundreds of older parent-documents, many of which belonged to earliest Christian times. Somehow this fact has to be explained; and it is not at all satisfactory to persist in arguing – against mounting evidence – that the Byzantine text does not appear in history until the fourth century. This text is early. It became widespread because it faithfully represented the original.

6. *Providential care has always been exercised towards God's Truth, because believers have needed that Truth in an accurate and correct form* (Matthew 24:35; 1 Peter 1:23,25). Hence, the Word given by inspiration has been the same as that subsequently published (Psalm 68:11). It is inconceivable that God would give a totally corrupt and mutilated text to His people and then allow that text to be used by them for over eighteen centuries. Yet that is exactly what some modern textual critics would have us believe! "Let it be remembered", writes Dr. Owen, "that the vulgar copy we use (The Received Text) was the public possession of many generations…; let that, then, pass for the standard, which is confessedly its right and due, and we shall, God assisting, quickly see how little reason there is to pretend such varieties of readings as we are now surprised withal".[22]

7. It is reasonable to suppose that *God acted similarly with respect to the texts of the Old and New Testaments.* His method with the Old Testament was to preserve the text, in a practically unaltered form, through many generations. The result – as Christ and His apostles clearly taught – was a Book in which every letter and part of a letter was sacred (Matthew 5:18; cf. John 10:35). When this ancient revelation was supplemented, God proceeded in the same way: He infallibly recorded His latest Word, placed it in the possession of His Church, and then *ensured that it was passed on through succeeding centuries, even to this present time.* "The word of the Lord…liveth and abideth for ever" (1 Peter 1:25).

B. *The Alexandrian Text-type*

This is a very small group of manuscripts. Peculiarities of spelling show that they are to be associated with Alexandria in Egypt; and, not surprisingly, readings from this type of text are to be found among the early Egyptian papyri (e.g., P46, P47). Its chief representatives, however, are Codex Sinaiticus (or Codex Aleph) and Codex Vaticanus (or Codex B).

Support for this text-type comes from the Alexandrian Fathers, most notably from Origen (AD 185-254) and Cyril (376-444).

Several things should be observed here:

1. This text-type *originated from Alexandria, in Egypt.* Scripture gives no indication that there was ever an apostolic presence in those parts, but church history reveals that many notorious heretics lived and taught there including such Gnostics as Basilides, Isidore, and Valentinus. Anything proceeding from this place must be regarded with some suspicion.

2. There is *clear evidence of revision* by its rearrangement of words. B.H. Streeter suggested that the editor was an Egyptian bishop called Hesychius.[23] This means that although great claims are made for it, this text-type cannot be regarded as singularly "pure".

3. The two great representatives of this text-type, Codices Aleph (Sinaiticus) and B (Vaticanus) are *exceedingly poor in quality*. When examined by Dr. F.H.A. Scrivener, Codex Aleph was declared to be "roughly written" and "full of gross transcriptural blunders" such as "leaving out whole lines of the original". Codex B, although "less faulty", was found to be "liable to err" committing "errors of the most palpable character".[24]

4. These principal manuscripts show their corruptions by *disagreeing with themselves in literally thousands of places* (3,000 times in the Gospels alone).

5. The text attested by Aleph (Sinaiticus) and B (Vaticanus) is *at variance with the overwhelming majority of the Greek manuscripts*. Not only is it confined to a very small family of manuscripts, but it has been estimated that there are somewhere in the region of 6,000 differences between the Alexandrian and Byzantine texts.

6. It is true that there is severe loss of text in B (Vaticanus), but considering their age (mid- or late-fourth century), these two uncials are in remarkably fine condition. Since most accurate manuscripts of this age perished through reason of use, it may be supposed that these were *rejected as flawed* and therefore were *not used by the early church*.

7. Supporting this conclusion is the fact that *very few copies indeed were made from them*. As stated by Dr. Gordon Clark, "If a score or two manuscripts have a single ancestor, it implies that a score or two copyists believed that ancestor to be faithful to the autographs. But if a manuscript has not a numerous progeny, as is the case with B's ancestor, one may suspect that the early scribes doubted its value. Possibly the early orthodox Christians knew that B was corrupt."[25]

CRITICS ATTACK THE BYZANTINE TEXT

In the last century, two Cambridge scholars, B.F. Westcott and F.J.A. Hort, elaborated *a radical new theory* about the early transmission of the New Testament text. They argued that the best text was actually the Alexandrian (which they called the "Neutral Text") represented by Aleph and B. Since those two manuscripts were slightly earlier than others, they claimed that their common ancestor was close to the inspired original. While absolute purity was not ascribed to this text, Westcott and Hort were prepared to say, "It is our belief (1) the readings of Aleph B should be accepted as the true readings until strong internal evidence is found to the contrary, and (2) that no readings of Aleph B can safely be rejected absolutely, though it is sometimes right to place them only on an alternative footing, especially where they receive no support from Versions or Fathers".[26]

The Byzantine text (called the "Syrian Text") contained, as they thought, "conflate readings", i.e., combinations of earlier readings; and they believed they originated in a two-stage revision produced at or near Antioch in the fourth century. Admitting this to be only "supposition", they advanced the view that "the growing diversity and confusion of Greek texts led to an authoritative revision at Antioch" and later "to a second authoritative revision". The whole process, according to them, was completed by 350 AD; and they even put forward the suggestion that Lucian of Antioch (martyred in 312) may have been involved in the earlier revision.

The theory is seriously flawed. Although critics and versions still refer to "the oldest and best manuscripts", the phrase is altogether misleading because, in this particular debate, the "oldest" are in fact the "worst". As for "conflate readings" in the Byzantine text, convincing evidence in support of them has never been produced (even after twenty-eight years of study Westcott and Hort could produce only eight examples). Anyway, long readings do not prove a later interference with the text. Professor Sturz has shown that some of these readings are supported by the earliest papyri (the longer readings of John 10:19 and 10:31, for example, are supported by P66).[27] This leads to the conclusion that the fault lies with the Alexandrian text. It stands accused of shortening the Byzantine text. What then of the so-called "Lucianic Recension"? There is no evidence that it ever took place.

Westcott and Hort set about the task of preparing a revised Greek text. It so happens that they were also members of the committee, appointed by the Convocation of Canterbury in 1880, to prepare a revised edition of the English Bible. Although their Greek text was not yet published, a proof copy was made available to the revisers; and when in 1881 the New Testament of the Revised Version appeared, it was immediately apparent that Westcott and Hort's Greek text had not only greatly influenced the committee but that it had also been generally followed in the Revised Version of the English New Testament.

This Westcott/Hort Text was the forerunner of what is known today as the Nestle/Aland (United Bible Societies) Text, which has usurped the place of the Byzantine or Traditional Text and subsequently formed the basis for practically all modern versions. The New International Version, for example, while claiming in its preface to follow an 'eclectic' Greek text (i.e., one compiled from a variety of manuscripts), proceeds at once to inform the reader that "where existing manuscripts differ, the translators made their choice of readings according to the accepted principles of New Testament textual criticism". Adoption of fundamentally flawed 'principles' has meant that the resultant text is very similar to the one produced in 1881 by Westcott and Hort.

The Authorised Version

During the Reformation and Puritan periods, a number of Protestant versions appeared, all based on the same authentic texts and translated according to the same valid principles.

In 1611, the Authorised Version was published and it was destined to supersede all its rivals. Like the earlier English versions – and versions of the same era in other languages – this used the providentially preserved *Hebrew Massoretic Text* and *Greek Received Text* (from the Byzantine family). The translators, justly famed for their godliness and scholarship, carried out their work with meticulous care. As a result, they produced a most faithful and accurate translation, still unrivalled in its majestic style, simplicity, and power. Indeed, such is this version's intrinsic worth that it has been called "the most excellent book in our language".

Modern versions come and they go, for which we are thankful. This version maintains its reputation, even against keen competitors like *The New King James Version*.

The Authorised Version, proven through the centuries and greatly loved by the Lord's people, is a truly noble production and it remains the best English translation of God's infallible and inerrant Word.

Malcolm Watts, a member of the General Committee of the Trinitarian Bible Society, was born in 1946 in Barnstaple, North Devon, England. Brought up in a Christian home, he was called by grace in his teenage years and, subsequently, called into the ministry. He trained at London Bible College between 1967-70, and since 1971 has been the minister of Emmanuel Church, Salisbury. He and Gillian were wed in 1976, and they have two daughters, Lydia and Naomi.

Endnotes

[1] James Bannerman, *Inspiration: the Infallible Truth and Divine Authority of the Holy Scriptures* (Edinburgh: T & T Clark, 1865), p. 158.

[2] Louis Gaussen, *Divine Inspiration of the Bible* (Grand Rapids: Kregel Publications, 1971. Published in Edinburgh in 1842 under the title, *Theopneustia: The Bible, its Divine Origin and Entire Inspiration, Deduced from Internal Evidence and the Testimonies of Nature, History, and Science*), p. 34.

[3] This was the view of the older commentators, Piscator, Poole, Clarke, Gill, and others. More recently, it has been maintained by Dr. Greg L. Bahnsen in "The Inerrancy of the Autographa", a chapter included in the symposium entitled *Inerrancy*, edited by Dr. Norman L. Geisler (Grand Rapids: Zondervan Publishing House, 1980), p. 167.

[4] William Henry Green, *General Introduction to the Old Testament: The Canon* (London: John Murray, 1899), p. 11.

[5] Further information on the state of the text at this period may be found in John H. Skilton, "The Transmission of the Scriptures", in *The Infallible Word, a Symposium by the Members of the Faculty of Westminster Theological Seminary*, third revised printing (Philadelphia: Presbyterian and Reformed Publishing Company, 1967) pp. 153ff. See also Thomas Hartwell Horne, *An Introduction to the Critical Study and Knowledge of the Holy Scriptures*, seventh edition, (London: T. Cadell, 1834), 2:34.

[6] Roger Nicole, "New Testament Use of the Old Testament", in *Revelation and the Bible*, Carl F.H. Henry, ed. (London: The Tyndale Press, 1959), pp. 142-43. See also the comments by Walter C. Kaiser Jnr, *The Uses of the Old Testament in the New* (Chicago: Moody Press, 1985), pp. 4ff.

[7] Skilton, p. 143.

[8] The Ante-Nicene Fathers, *Tertullian, On Prescription against Heretics*, chap. 36 (Grand Rapids: William Eerdmans Publishing Company, 1979), 3:260.

[9] Dr A. Cleveland Coxe, who edited Tertullian's works for the original Edinburgh edition, concedes in a footnote that the "much disputed phrase ('their own authentic writings') may refer to the autographs or the Greek originals". However, he thinks that "probably" the reference is to "full unmutilated copies". Edward Miller (who edited several of Dean Burgon's works), appears to have believed that Tertullian was alluding to the original manuscripts. He wrote: "Tertullian, in arguing with heretics, bids them consult the autographs of the Apostles at Corinth, or Thessalonica, or Ephesus, or Rome, where they are preserved and read in public" (*A Guide to the Textual Criticism of the New Testament* [London: George Bell and Sons, 1886], p. 72).

[10] The Ante-Nicene Fathers, *Polycarp, The Epistle of Polycarp to the Philippians*, chap. 12, 1:35.

[11] J.P. Lilley, *The Pastoral Epistles* (Edinburgh: T & T Clark, 1901), p. 216.

[12] Caspar Rene Gregory, *Canon and Text of the New Testament* (Edinburgh: T. & T. Clark, 1907), p. 309. Dr Gregory comments: "No one will imagine...that only those letters and not the book of Revelation were to be sent to the churches, for that verse (Revelation 1:11) says that John is to write in the book what he sees, that is to say the visions which follow, and send it to the churches" (p. 310).

[13] The Ecclesiastical History and Martyrs of Palestine, *Eusebius, Ecclesiastical History*, book 3, chap. 37. (London: Society for Promoting Christian Knowledge, 1928).

[14] Ibid., book 4, chap. 23.

[15] Ibid., book 5, chap. 28.

[16] Tertullian, chap. 38, 3:262.

[17] The Ante-Nicene Fathers, *Irenaeus, Irenaeus against Heresies*, book 5, chap. 30, sect. 1, 1:558.

[18] Kurt and Barbara Aland, *The Text of the New Testament: an Introduction to the Critical Editions and to the Theory and Practice of Modern Textual Criticism*, 2nd ed, 1989. Cited by Bruce M. Metzger in *The Text of the New Testament: Its Transmission, Corruption, and Restoration*, third, enlarged edition (Oxford: Oxford University Press, 1992), p. 262.

[19] Benjamin B. Warfield, *An Introduction to the Textual Criticism of the New Testament* (London: Hodder and Stoughton, 1886), pp. 110, 111.

[20] Harry A. Sturz, *The Byzantine Text-Type and New Testament Textual Criticism* (Nashville, TN: Thomas Nelson Publishers, 1984), pp. 61ff, 145ff.

[21] Edward Miller in "The Antiquity of the Traditional Text", in John William Burgon, *The Traditional Text of the Holy Gospels Vindicated and Established* (London: George Bell and Sons, 1896), p. 121.

[22] John Owen, "Of the Integrity and Purity of the Hebrew and Greek Text of the Scripture", in *The Works of John Owen* (London: The Banner of Truth Trust, 1968), 16:366.

[23] B.H. Streeter, *The Four Gospels: A Study of Origins*, revised from the 1924 edition (London: Macmillan & Co. Ltd, 1956), pp. 112ff, 121ff.

[24] F.H.A. Scrivener, *Six Lectures on the Text of the New Testament and the Ancient Manuscripts* (Cambridge: Deighton, Bell, and Co., 1875), pp. 41, 43.

[25] Gordon H. Clark, *Logical Criticisms of Textual Criticism* (Jefferson, MD: The Trinity Foundation, 1986), p. 15.

[26] B.F. Westcott and F.J.A. Hort, *Introduction to the New Testament in the Original Greek* (Massachusetts: Hendrickson Publishers, 1988. Originally published by Harper and Brothers, New York, 1882), p. 225.

[27] Sturz, p. 84.